THE LITTLE BOOK OF COMPASSION

Parts of this book were first published in 2020 by Trigger, an imprint of Shaw Callaghan Ltd.

This expanded edition published in 2023 by OH! an Imprint of Welbeck Non-Fiction Limited, part of Welbeck Publishing Group.
Offices in: London – 20 Mortimer Street, London W1T 3JW
and Sydney – 205 Commonwealth Street, Surry Hills 2010
www.welbeckpublishing.com

Disclaimer:
OH! encourages diversity and different viewpoints. However, all views, thoughts, and opinions expressed in this book are not necessarily representative of Welbeck Publishing Group as an organization. All material in this book is set out in good faith for general guidance; no liability can be accepted for loss or expense incurred in following the information given. In particular, this book is not intended to replace expert medical or phychiatric advice. It is intended for informational purposes only and for your own personal use and guidance. It is not intended to diagnose, treat or act as a substitute for professional medical advice.

ISBN 978-1-80069-354-8

Editorial: Victoria Denne
Project manager: Russell Porter
Production: Jess Brisley

A CIP catalogue record for this book is available from the British Library

Printed in China

10 9 8 7 6 5 4 3 2 1

THE LITTLE BOOK OF

COMPASSION

FOR WHEN LIFE
GETS A LITTLE TOUGH

CONTENTS

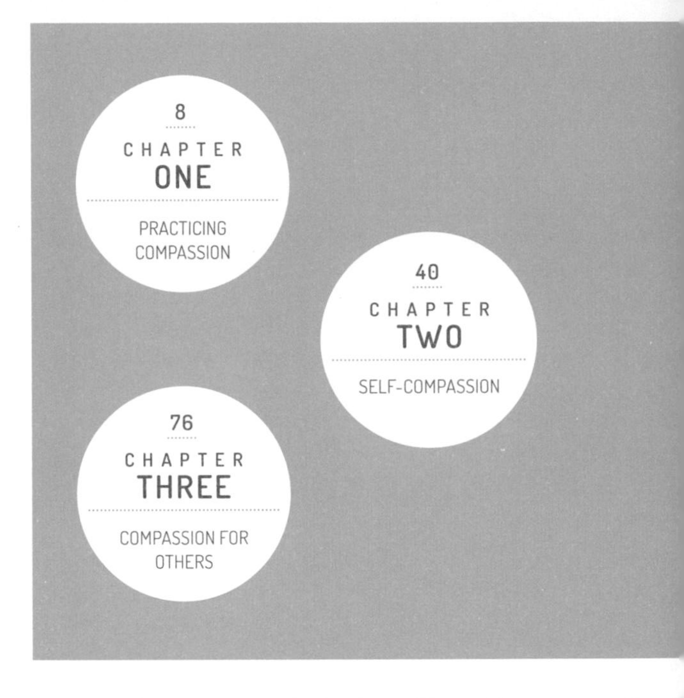

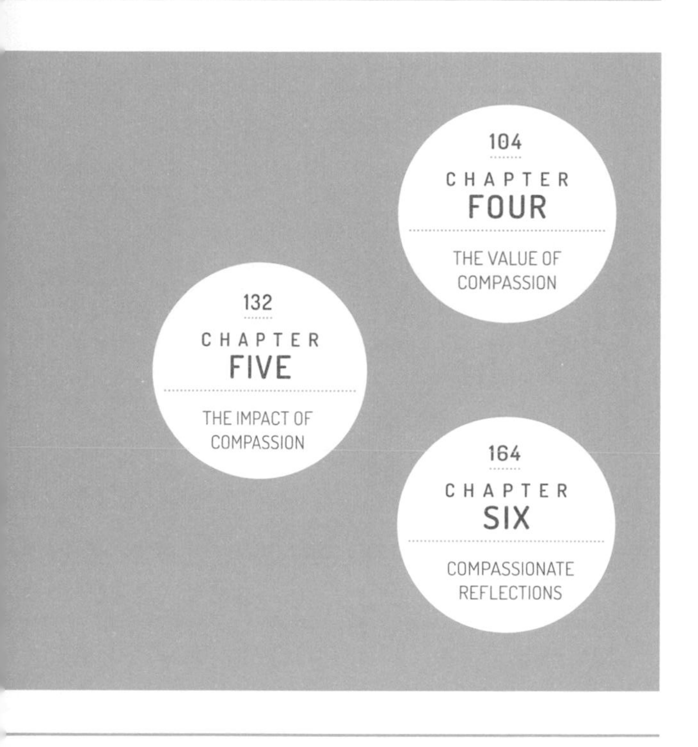

INTRODUCTION

The virtue of compassion is universally valued. Derived from the Latin "com" and "passio" and meaning "to suffer together", practicing compassion can strengthen your relationships, lessen the grip of negative thoughts, and increase emotional resilience. But how can we lean into loving kindness and cultivate compassion every day?

The Little Book of Compassion offers guidance from some of the world's greatest minds in the art of responding to ourselves and others with compassion and kindness in times of difficulty. For true compassion allows us to diminish our indifference to the suffering around us.

CHAPTER 1

PRACTICING COMPASSION

By connecting more deeply with the world, fostering greater emotional intelligence, and practicing kindness, we can cultivate compassion to help ourselves and those around us.

Real living is living for others.

Bruce Lee

We must learn to regard people less in the light of what they do or omit to do, and more in the light of what they suffer.

Dietrich Bonhoeffer

“

I tell my students, ‘When you get these jobs that you have been so brilliantly trained for, just remember that your real job is that if you are free, you need to free somebody else. If you have some power, then your job is to empower somebody else. This is not just a grab-bag candy game.'

Toni Morrison

When people talk, listen completely.
Most people never listen.

Ernest Hemingway

In compassion, when we feel with the other, we dethrone ourselves from the centre of our world and we put another person there.

Karen Armstrong

When you like someone, you like them in spite of their faults. When you love someone, you love them with their faults.

Hermann Hesse

There is no exercise better
for the heart than reaching down
and lifting people up.

John Holmes

Love and compassion are
necessities, not luxuries.
Without them, humanity
cannot survive.

Dalai Lama

That's what I consider true generosity: You give your all, and yet you always feel as if it costs you nothing.

Simone de Beauvoir

“

One of the most spiritual things you can do is embrace your humanity. Connect with those around you today. Say, ‘I love you’, ‘I’m sorry’, ‘I appreciate you’,

'I'm proud of you', whatever you're feeling. Send random texts, write a cute note, embrace your truth and share it.

Steve Maraboli

If a man cannot understand
the beauty of life, it is probably
because life never understood
the beauty in him.

Criss Jami

No act of kindness, no matter how small, is ever wasted.

Aesop

People take different roads seeking fulfilment and happiness. Just because they're not on your road doesn't mean they've gotten lost.

Dalai Lama

Use your voice for kindness, your ears for compassion, your hands for charity, your mind for truth, and your heart for love.

Anonymous

“

If a person seems wicked, do not cast him away. Awaken him with your words, elevate him with your deeds, repay his injury with your

kindness. Do not cast him away;
cast away his wickedness.

Lao-Tzu

Compassion is the wish to see others free from suffering.

Dalai Lama

I feel like if you're a really good human being, you can try to find something beautiful in every single person, no matter what.

Lady Gaga

Carry out a random act of kindness, with no expectation of reward, safe in the knowledge that one day someone might do the same for you.

Princess Diana

Your need for acceptance can make you invisible in this world. Don't let anything stand in the way of the light that shines through this form. Risk being seen in all of your glory.

Jim Carrey

Unexpected kindness is the most powerful, least costly, and most underrated agent of human change.

Bob Kerrey

Love and kindness are never wasted.
They always make a difference.
They bless the one who receives
them, and they bless you, the giver.

Barbara De Angelis

Strong people don't put others down. They lift them up.

Michael P. Watson

You cannot do kindness too soon, for you never know how soon it will be too late.

Ralph Waldo Emerson

“

Too often we underestimate the power of a touch, a smile, a kind word, a listening ear, an honest compliment, or the smallest act of caring, all of which have the potential to turn a life around.

Leo Buscaglia

Kindness begins with the understanding that we all struggle.

Charles Glassman

There is no small act of kindness.
Every compassionate act makes
large the world.

Mary Anne Radmacher

CHAPTER 2

SELF-COMPASSION

Achieving a state of complete self-acceptance when we suffer, fail, or feel inadequate isn't always easy. Learning to comfort oneself in the moment is a vital part of showing self-compassion.

Be good to yourself 'cause nobody else has the power to make you happy.

George Michael

You've been criticizing yourself for years and it hasn't worked. Try approving of yourself and see what happens.

Louise L. Hay

It doesn't matter who you are,
where you come from; the ability to
triumph begins with you – always.

Oprah Winfrey

To be a great champion you
must believe you are the best.
If you're not, pretend you are.

Muhammad Ali

Both men and women should feel free to be sensitive. Both men and women should feel free to be strong.

Emma Watson

“

Whatever the present moment contains,
accept it as if you had chosen it.

Eckhart Tolle

“

It’s difficult to believe in yourself because the idea of self is an artificial construction. You are, in fact, part of the glorious oneness of

the universe. Everything beautiful
in the world is within you.

Russell Brand

I know what I can do,
so I never doubt myself.

Usain Bolt

This is a moment of suffering. Suffering is part of life. May I be kind to myself in this moment. May I give myself the compassion I need.

Kristin Neff

Love and compassion are
necessities, not luxuries.
Without them humanity
cannot survive.

Dalai Lama

Mistakes are always forgivable,
if one has the courage to admit them.

Bruce Lee

You can't let your failures define you. You have to let your failures teach you.

Barack Obama

Eventually you just have to realize that you're living for an audience of one. I'm not here for anyone else's approval.

Pamela Anderson

“

There's only one of you, so why would you want to look like everyone else? Why would you want to have the same hairstyle as everyone else

and have the same opinions as
everybody else?

Adele

“

You have this one life. How do you wanna spend it? Apologizing? Regretting? Questioning? Hating yourself? Dieting? Running after people who don’t see you?

Be brave. Believe in yourself.
Do what feels good. Take risks.
You have this one life. Make
yourself proud.

Cara Delevingne

I have my flaws, but I embrace them and I love them because they're mine.

Winnie Harlow

Success is liking yourself, liking what you do, and liking how you do it.

Maya Angelou

You're only given a little spark
of madness. You mustn't lose it.

Robin Williams

Desperation is a necessary ingredient to learning anything, or creating anything. Period. If you ain't desperate at some point, you ain't interesting.

Jim Carrey

If your compassion does not include yourself, it is incomplete.

Demi Lovato

You deserve the best, the very best, because you are one of the few people in this lousy world who are honest to themselves, and that is the only thing that really counts.

Frida Khalo

I was once afraid of people saying
'Who does she think she is?'
Now I have the courage to stand
and say 'This is who I am.'

Oprah Winfrey

I don't want to have plastic surgery.
I'm going to look like this forever.
Deal with it. Once you deal with it,
you feel more calm about it.

Adele

“

Being human is not about being any one particular way; it is about being as life creates you – with your own particular strengths and

weaknesses, gifts and challenges,
quirks and oddities.

Kristin Neff

I'm not perfect ... But I'm enough.

Carl R. Rogers

If you do not respect your own wishes, no one else will. You will simply attract people who disrespect you as much as you do.

Vironika Tugaleva

"

It is a beautiful experience being with ourselves at a level of complete acceptance. When that begins to happen, when you give up resistance and needing to be perfect, a peace will come over you as you have never known.

Ruth Fishel

The privilege of a lifetime
is being who you are.

Joseph Campbell

Self-compassion is simply giving the same kindness to ourselves that we would give to others.

Christopher Germer

CHAPTER 3

COMPASSION FOR OTHERS

Be mindful of the needs of others, as well as your own. Offering a hug or a word of understanding in a moment of crisis can positively change the perspective of those in a vulnerable mental state.

Be kind, for everyone you meet
is fighting a hard battle.

Plato

We never know the journey
another person has walked,
so be kind to everyone.

Lynette Mather

For me, I am driven by two main philosophies: know more today about the world than I knew yesterday and lessen the suffering of others. You'd be surprised how far that gets you.

Neil deGrasse Tyson

“

Compassion is an unstable emotion. It needs to be translated into action, or it withers.

Susan Sontag

“

What’s important is to be able to see yourself, I think, as having commonality with other people and not determine, because of

your good luck, that everybody
is less significant, less interesting,
less important than you are.

Harrison Ford

Every life deserves a certain amount of dignity, no matter how poor or damaged the shell that carries it.

Rick Bragg

This planet is for everyone;
borders are for no one.
It's all about freedom.

Benjamin Zephaniah

Society's punishments are
small compared to the wounds
we inflict on our soul when
we look the other way.

Martin Luther King Jr.

Give the ones you love wings
to fly, roots to come back, and
reasons to stay.

Dalai Lama

Let no one ever come to you
without leaving happier.

Mother Teresa

I always just thought if you
see somebody without a smile,
give 'em yours!

Dolly Parton

“

Everybody can be great ... because anybody can serve. You don’t have to have a college degree to serve. You don’t have to make your subject and verb agree to serve. You only need a heart full of grace. A soul generated by love.

Martin Luther King Jr.

“

You know it’s love when all you want is that person to be happy, even if you’re not part of their happiness.

Julia Roberts

”

“

There's nothing greater in the world than when somebody on the team does something good, and everybody gathers around to pat him on the back.

Billy Martin

“

The gentle and sensitive companionship of an empathic stance ... provides illumination and healing. In such situations deep

understanding is, I believe,
the most precious gift one can
give to another.

Carl R. Rogers

A part of kindness consists in loving people more than they deserve.

Joseph Joubert

The only way out of the labyrinth
of suffering is to forgive.

John Green

When the other person is hurting, confused, troubled, anxious, alienated, terrified; or when he or she is doubtful of self-worth, uncertain as to identity, then understanding is called for.

Carl R. Rogers

We have to make mistakes; it's how we learn compassion for others.

Curtis Sittenfeld

We are all different. Don't judge, understand instead.

Roy T. Bennett

No one has ever become
poor by giving.

Anne Frank

Our task must be to free ourselves... by widening our circle of compassion to embrace all living creatures and the whole of nature and its beauty.

Albert Einstein

If it is not tempered by compassion, and empathy, reason can lead men and women into a moral void.

Karen Armstrong

CHAPTER 4

THE VALUE OF COMPASSION

Showing compassion for another human being is priceless. The emotional rewards and societal benefits are reaped by the giver, the recipient, and the wider community.

Every day, you have the power to choose our better history by opening your hearts and minds, by speaking up for what you know is right.

Michelle Obama

Do not judge me by my successes, judge me by how many times I fell down and got back up again.

Nelson Mandela

We may have all come on
different ships, but we're in
the same boat now.

Martin Luther King Jr.

Forgiveness is not an occasional act;
it is a constant attitude.

Martin Luther King Jr.

I think love is unconditional; you find someone that you can grow with and that makes you want to grow and makes you a better person.

Channing Tatum

I speak to everyone in the same way, whether he is the garbage man or the president of the university.

Albert Einstein

Forgiveness liberates the soul.
It removes fear. That is why it is
such a powerful weapon.

Nelson Mandela

Talent wins games, but teamwork and intelligence win championships.

Michael Jordan

“

You need to be aware of what others are doing, applaud their efforts, acknowledge their successes and encourage them

in their pursuits. When we all help
one another, everybody wins.

Jim Stovall

There's nothing better than a world where everybody's just trying to make each other laugh.

Matthew Perry

Love is the most powerful force in the universe, and we have the extraordinary ability to give and receive it.

Tim A. Ewell

“

The hardest thing for not only
an artist but for anybody to do is
look themselves in the mirror and
acknowledge, you know, their own

flaws and fears and imperfections
and put them out there in the
open for people to relate to it.

Kendrick Lamar

You deserve a lover who listens when you sing, who supports you when you feel shame and respects your freedom.

Frida Khalo

Being deeply loved by someone gives you strength, while loving someone deeply gives you courage.

Lao Tzu

“

Highly sensitive people are too often perceived as weaklings or damaged goods. To feel intensely is not a symptom of weakness.

It is the trademark of the truly alive and compassionate.

Anthon St. Maarten

A kind gesture can reach a wound that only compassion can heal.

Steve Maraboli

When we match compassion with purpose, we begin to change the world.

Zachariah Thompson

Life is an exciting business, and most exciting when it is lived for others.

Helen Keller

When we give cheerfully and accept gratefully, everyone is blessed.

Maya Angelou

Humanity's collective mission
in the cosmos lies in the practice
of compassion.

Dalsaku Ikeda

Compassion will cure more sins than condemnation.

Henry Ward Beecher

“

When a person realizes he has been deeply heard, his eyes moisten. I think in some real sense he is weeping for joy. It is as though he were saying 'Thank God, somebody heard me. Someone knows what it's like to be me'.

Carl R. Rogers

CHAPTER 5

THE IMPACT OF COMPASSION

The ability to see things from someone else's perspective and sympathize with their emotions enables us to better understand how to relieve the suffering of ourselves and others.

Remember there's no such thing as a small act of kindness. Every act creates a ripple with no logical end.

.Scott Adams

To love is to recognize
yourself in another.

Eckhart Tolle

There are things in my life that
are hard to reconcile, like divorce.
Sometimes it is very difficult to
make sense of how it could possibly
happen. Laying blame is so easy. I
don't have time for hate or negativity
in my life. There's no room for it.

Reese Witherspoon

Someone I once loved gave
me a box full of darkness. It took
me years to understand that
this, too, was a gift.

Mary Oliver

Beauty is not who you are on the outside, it is the wisdom and time you gave away to save another struggling soul like you.

Shannon L. Alder

Often, it is the most deserving people who cannot help loving those who destroy them.

Herman Hesse

“

No one is born hating another person because of the color of his skin, or his background, or his religion. People must learn to hate, and if they can learn to hate they can be taught to love, for love comes more naturally to the human heart than its opposite.

Nelson Mandela

Kind words can be short and easy to speak, but their echoes are truly endless.

Mother Teresa

For me, success is a state of mind. I feel like success isn't about conquering something; it's being happy with who you are.

Britney Spears

“

I’ve been angry. I’ve been incredibly angry and hurt. But I’ve come to realise that I’m not defined by my scars, but by the

incredible ability to heal, and
forgiveness is part of healing.

Lemn Sissay

Weakness is something we don't like to admit we have. We hold it against people, until we experience it, and then we feel more compassion for it.

Olivia Wilde

I used to think that confidence
came from what other people
thought about me but now
I realize it comes from what
I feel about myself.

Demi Lovato

“

There is no such thing as a self-made man. You will reach your goals only with the help of others.

George Shinn

All the adversity I've had in my life, all my troubles and obstacles, have strengthened me ... You may not realize it when it happens but a kick in the teeth may be the best thing in the world for you.

Walt Disney

More smiling, less worrying.
More compassion, less judgement.
More blessed, less stressed.
More love, less hate.

Roy T. Bennet

Empathy for other people's feelings requires a counter-balancing quality of toughness to not be controlled by their pain.

Al Siebert

At the end of the day, we can endure much more than we think we can.

Frida Khalo

Kindness in words creates
confidence. Kindness in thinking
creates profoundness.
Kindness in giving creates love.

Lao Tzu

That is what compassion does.
It challenges our assumptions,
our sense of self-limitation,
worthlessness, of not having a
place in the world. As we develop
compassion, our hearts open.

Sharon Salzberg

The light of compassion opens
the petals of the heart. When the
petals of the heart unfold, fragrance
spreads across the valley.

Amit Ray

“

Learning to stand in somebody else's shoes, to see through their eyes, that's how peace begins. And it's up to you to make that happen. Empathy is a quality of character that can change the world.

Barack Obama

One of the most important things you can do on this earth is to let people know they are not alone.

Shannon L. Alder

If you want more kindness in the world, put some there.

Zero Dean

When you show deep empathy toward others, their defensive energy goes down, and positive energy replaces it. That's when you can get more creative in solving problems.

Stephen Covey

Walk with me for a while, my friend – you in my shoes, I in yours – and then let us talk.

Richelle E. Goodrich

Empathy is the gateway;
compassion is the way.

Scott Perry

One does not remember
one's own pain. It is the suffering
of others that undoes us.

Anna Funder

CHAPTER 6

COMPASSIONATE REFLECTIONS

Guided by some of the world's greatest minds, here are some thought-provoking reflections on the importance of showing compassion and tips on how to implement the practice every day.

“

Everybody is a genius. But if you judge a fish by its ability to climb a tree, it will live its whole life believing that it is stupid.

Albert Einstein

Nothing would mean anything if
I didn't live a life of use to others.

Angelina Jolie

Art is to console those
who are broken by life.

Vincent Van Gogh

You define beauty yourself,
society doesn't define your beauty.

Lady Gaga

Hating people because of their colour is wrong. And it doesn't matter which colour does the hating. It's just plain wrong.

Muhammad Ali

None of us is as smart as all of us.

Ken Blanchard

Our primary purpose is to help others. And if you can't help them, at least don't hurt them.

Dalai Lama

Save one-third, live on one-third,
and give away one-third.

Angelina Jolie

“

It is good to love many things,
for therein lies the true strength,
and whosoever loves much
performs much and can

accomplish much, and what is
done in love is well done.

Vincent Van Gogh

Compassion and tolerance are not a sign of weakness, but a sign of strength.

Dalai Lama

Sometimes it takes only one act of kindness and caring to change a person's life.

Jackie Chan

“

Compassion is at the heart of every little thing we do. It is the dearest quality we possess. Yet all too often it can be cast aside with consequences too tragic to speak of. To lose our compassion, we lose what it is to be human.

Anonymous

We can't heal the world today
but we can begin with a voice of
compassion, a heart of love,
an act of kindness.

Mary Davis

Having compassion starts and ends with having compassion for all those unwanted parts of ourselves.

Pema Chodron

Taking time to relax every day, spending quality time with friends, and practicing mindfulness are some of the tried and tested ways of developing self-compassion.

Dr. Prem Jagyasi

Love and compassion are the
mother and father of a smile.
We need to create more smiles in
our world today. Smiles, after all,
pave the way to a happy world.

Steve Maraboli

Grief can be the garden of
compassion. If you keep your
heart open through everything,
your pain can become your

greatest ally in your life's search
for love and wisdom.

Rumi

Love and compassion are the true religions to me. But to develop this, we do not need to believe in any religion.

Dalai Lama

One's life has value so long as one attributes value to the life of others, by means of love, friendship, indignation and compassion.

Simone de Beauvoir

True compassion means not
only feeling another's pain but
also being moved to help relieve it.

Daniel Goleman

It is not until you become a mother that your judgement slowly turns to compassion and understanding.

Erma Bombeck

“

There is nothing heavier than
compassion. Not even one's
own pain weighs so heavy as
the pain one feels for someone,

with someone, pain intensified
by the imagination and
prolonged by a hundred echoes.

Milan Kundera

I would rather make mistakes
in kindness and compassion
than work miracles in unkindness
and hardness.

Mother Teresa